Our Father

Our Father

Meditations on the Lord's Prayer

RUTH BURROWS

Edited by ELIZABETH RUTH OBBARD

Dimension Books Inc.
Denville, N.J. 07834

First U.S.A. edition by Dimension Books Inc.
P.O. Box 811, Denville, N.J. 07834 through
arrangement with Darton, Longman and Todd Ltd, London

© 1986 Ruth Burrows

ISBN 0-87193-255-5
All rights reserved

Phototypeset by
Input Typesetting Ltd,
London SW19 8DR
Printed and bound in Great Britain by
Anchor Brendon Ltd, Tiptree, Essex

My Father
and your Father,
My God
  and your God
    (John 20:17)

Contents

Acknowledgements

The introduction was first published as 'Growth in Prayer', in *The Way* (October 1983), and is reproduced with the Editor's permission.

The biblical quotations in the introduction are mostly taken from the Revised Standard Version, copyrighted 1971 and 1952 by the Division of Christian Education of the National Council of the Churches of Christ in the USA; those in the text are mostly from the New Jerusalem Bible, published and copyright 1985 by Darton, Longman and Todd Ltd and Doubleday and Company Inc., and are used by permission of the publishers.

Editor's Preface

Imagine that the Lord Himself is at your side and see how lovingly and how humbly He is teaching you (the Our Father) . . . If you become accustomed to having Him at your side, and if He sees that you love Him to be there and are always trying to please Him, you will never be able, as we put it, to send Him away, nor will He ever fail you. He will help you in all your trials and you will have Him everywhere. Do you think it is a small thing to have such a friend as that beside you?[1]

St Teresa of Avila described the Christian's life of prayer as a life of friendship with Jesus. For her, prayer was the life-blood of the soul, and her one desire was to introduce others to a like intimacy with the Lord.

I feel the same can be said of Ruth Burrows. She understands in a unique way not only her own vocation as a Carmelite but the vocation of all men and women to whom God offers himself in the intimacy of prayer, whatever outward form their lives may take and however diverse their callings in the Church.

In these collected writings she patterns her teaching on Jesus' own prayer, the Our Father. He can teach us to pray as can no other, for his whole life was a continual prayer of love, praise, gratitude and surrender to the Father, whose only-begotten Son he knew himself to be.

My hope is that these short meditations will introduce many to the riches hidden in the Lord's Prayer

[1] St Teresa, *Way of Perfection*, XXVI.

9

and encourage them to persevere with great trust, however dark and unrewarding the way of prayer may seem on the natural level. With Jesus they are being asked to surrender to the Spirit and become a son in the Son. For:

> Everyone moved by the Spirit is a son of God. The spirit you received is not the spirit of slaves . . . it is the spirit of sons, and it makes us cry out, 'Abba, Father!' The Spirit himself and our spirit bear united witness that we are children of God. And if we are children we are heirs as well: heirs of God and co-heirs with Christ, sharing his sufferings so as to share his glory.[1]

ELIZABETH RUTH OBBARD

[1] Rom. 8:14–17.

Introduction

As soon as we would talk or write about prayer and growth in prayer we are faced with huge difficulties. We are talking and writing not merely about the deepest thing in human life but about its very essence – more, about the mystery of God himself. We are daring to use terms such as 'intimacy', 'friendship', for that we are called to such is beyond doubt for the believer. We find a breathing of it in the first pages of Genesis where, it is intimated, God was wont to walk with his man and woman through the garden in the cool of the day. Though sin came to rupture this blessed state, still, throughout the pages of the Old Testament with its history of humans as they really are – sinful, blind, obstinate, hard of heart – there shine stars, 'friends of God', who in some measure attained or were granted intimacy with the awful mystery. Such intimacy is still possible. Amidst a perverse and corrupt people 'Enoch walked with God; and he was not, for God took him'.[1] Here, it is suggested, was someone for whom God meant so much that he was swallowed up by him. Enoch disappeared, only God shone out. In this pregnant phrase of scripture we have a summing up of holiness, of the perfection of a human life.

Moses spoke with God face to face and through this terrible exposure was transformed in such a way that he became 'God' for the people at large, a people too sensual and selfish to want God himself. They were not prepared to pay the price.

[1] Gen. 5:24.

We have heard his voice out of the midst of the fire; we have this day seen God speak with man and man still alive. Now, therefore, why should we die? For this great fire will consume us; if we hear the voice of the Lord our God any more, we shall die. For who is there of all flesh, that has heard the voice of the living God speaking out of the midst of fire, as we have, and has still lived? Go near, and hear all that the Lord God will say; and speak to us all that the Lord our God will speak to you; and we will hear it and do it.[1]

This is an authentic human cry. If we use the term 'friendship with God' then we must know what we are doing, we must speak with utmost seriousness and with deep awe. There is no place for 'lightness', for trifling. What did it mean for Enoch, what did it mean for Moses – and, we shall ask, what did it mean for Jesus – to be a friend of God, to be on that lonely, dreadful mountain exposed to we know not what? And yet intimacy with God is the blissful fulfilment of us all. It is what we were made for and what we endlessly yearn for. It is to this that we blindly reach out in our human search for friendship and intimacy, but whereas even the richest human friendship, even that which has truly made of two one flesh, is only part of an existence and life; our relationship with God is our very meaning as human beings. Man – and that means you and me – is, by definition, a relation to God. We become human, become what we are meant to be, in the measure that, like Enoch of old, we are lost to ourselves and taken up into him. Prayer, on our side, is a conscious affirmation of this truth, an effective desire and willing that it be accomplished.

How do we attain to intimacy with God or rather, how do we enter into the intimacy offered? We must

[1] Deut. 5:24–7 RSV.

be certain that no wooing is necessary. We do not have to find ways of attracting the divine partner, of getting him to notice us. Here is someone who is love itself and the very fount of our own existence, enfolding us, inviting us to receive him, drawing us to his heart. All these human expressions are totally inadequate. Scripture and mystical writers have used the different modes of human love and friendship – parent/child, husband/wife, brother, friend – to tell us something of the reality of God's love and desire for us. Each is inadequate. All together they are inadequate. It is not easy to speak properly of a deep human relationship; how much more so when one of the partners is God! And even if one were able, through profound experience and intensive thought and effort, to give what seems as close a proximation to the truth as is possible, its understanding depends on the heart of the recipient. Truth must find an echo in the one who hears if it is to be recognised. Put it another way, a heart must be *really* listening, *really* wanting the truth, *really* wanting God. The difficulty is that we do not want him. We want our own version of him, one we can, so to speak, carry around in our pockets rather as some superstitious people carry around a charm. We can hold endless loving conversations with this one, feel we have an intimate understanding of him, we can tell him our troubles, ask for his approbation and admiration, consult him about all our affairs and decisions and get the answer we want, and this god of ours has almost nothing to do with God.

Most of us find it almost impossible not to think of prayer as a special activity in life, as an art that can be taught or learned rather as we can learn to play a musical instrument, and so some of us are quick to feel we are proficient and others that we are painfully handicapped, are missing out on some secret or have some lack in our nature which makes prayer difficult if not impossible for us. We feel there are certain laws governing

13

prayer, and techniques to be mastered, and when we have got hold of these we can pray. Thus we look around for the guru, for the one who has mastered the art and its techniques, and eagerly look to be taught. When we take up a book or article on prayer, we shall probably detect, if we stop to think, that we are looking for the key, the magic formula that is going to put our prayer right, enable us to 'make a go' of this mysterious activity called prayer. We may feel that others seem to take it in their stride but somehow it does not work for us and anxiously we look hither and thither for someone who will hand us the secret. All this is proof enough that we are overlooking the fundamental facts: that prayer is not a technique but a relationship; that there is no handicap, no obstacle, no problem. The only problem is that we do not want God. We may want a 'spiritual life', we may want 'prayer', but we do not want God. All anyone can do for us, any guru can teach us, is to keep our eyes on Jesus, God's perfect, absolute friend.

If we look at the gospels we shall find that Jesus never speaks to us as being friends of God. He teaches us to call him Father. Friend implies equality of status, child or son a total dependence and absolute obedience. When Jesus gave us his own privilege of calling God Abba, that word certainly carried with it everything we understand of the unbreakable, utterly reliable, tender, compassionate, infinitely involved fatherly/motherly love of God. Of this we must be sure to the marrow of our bones. But equally we must remember what the father-son relationship was in the Jewish culture of Jesus' time. We can go so far as to say that the son was considered as having no life or even existence of his own. He owed absolutely everything to the father: we might say a son was his father's 'thing', and the son owed him total, unconditional obedience. When Jesus tells us that we must call God Abba, and live as his children, he is demanding of us this decentralisation, this 'ex-stasy', this standing out of self, in order to transfer our existence, our meaning, our importance, our weight, to the Father. It is a summons to the most radical self-denial.

On the other hand Jesus gives us the title 'friend', his friend, in that we have opened ourselves to and received his revelation of the Father, that we trust him with our lives, obey him as Jesus did. To become the friend of Jesus means to identify with his living for his Father. This alone is prayer, this alone is intimacy with God. Its blissful fulfilment remains hidden from our sight and experience as it was for Jesus in his earthly life. All that concerns us here and now is what concerned Jesus: that God should have just whatever he wants. Jesus has become our way, our truth and our life because he declined to have any way of his own, any truth or reality of his own, only the Father's. He declined to live from his own well-springs but only from the Father. This is what we have to do; this is how we must live.

Jesus is with us always not so as to pillow our weary heads on his breast and murmur words of solace in our ears continually, but to share with us his vision, his passionate dedication to the Father's will. He is with us to brace, reinforce, underpin us for our life's great task. He lifts from our shoulders the crushing yoke of an alien master, the god we have fashioned in our own likeness, by revealing the true face of the Father. He breaks off self-made shackles of bondage and sets us free. Thus his companionship gives us rest and real happiness. Nevertheless there remains a yoke and a burden that has to be carried with courage and love.

Life-giving, joy-giving knowledge of Jesus and the Father he reveals does not drop into our lap from heaven. We have to work for it. 'Come to me', says Jesus, and we must go to him, and the prime way of going to him is by intent, loving absorption of scripture, particularly the New Testament. Put simply, we must strive to aquire an intellectual knowledge of him, of his attitudes, values, teaching. This intellectual knowledge is certainly not intimacy, certainly not a 'knowing Jesus' but it is an indispensable ingredient for intimacy and real knowing. It is work we have to do, a practical expression of earnest desire to get to know our Lord. Moreover it supplies, so to speak, the matter into which spirit can be infused, or in more homely words, we laboriously gather the faggots to build the bonfire which only God can set alight. But it has to be there for him to set alight. We must realise that it is not a case of our having to labour all by ourselves until the bonfire is a good size and everything well-dried out and then we can hope for God to set fire to it. No, we are never working alone. When we search for him in the scriptures we have already found him. He is with us, at a level we do not perceive and cannot perceive, touching our inmost depths and working within, infusing light, inflaming the will. From time to time we may be aware of enlightenment and a stirring of desire but it is utter folly to conclude that, if we do not feel those things 'it has not come off' and 'I am getting nowhere'. That might be so were we engaged in secular study or even in sacred scripture in a secular way, but it is certainly not so when we are 'listening' to the word of God be it in our private reflection or in the communal 'listening' of the liturgy. We are engaged in a sacramental action. Something is happening as it happens in the Eucharist and other sacraments. But as with them, our part is essential. We must bring our elements. 'Seek and you *will* find', Jesus assures us solemnly. Our seeking in scripture must be like that of the bride in the Canticles, all heart, never a merely intellectul effort. Our heart must infuse our minds with trust, desire, resolution. Our heart must be in our eyes as we read and in our ears as we hear. Most certainly then we shall find him.

This search for the beloved in the revealed word

means that our times of silent prayer have content. We have strong motives for perseverance. We have a growing though obscure knowledge of the Father before whom we are trustfully exposed. We can recognise him as he comes to us in our daily lives, quickly discern his demands with ever growing depth and clarity. We have his own vision by which to interpret the revelation of material creation and human history.

Jesus draws us to himself not for himself but so as to take us to the Father. The Father has asked him to be our friend. He has confided us to him as a cherished possession and Jesus considers us more precious than the whole world and his own life. Jesus was unimportant to himself. We are only his friends in truth if we allow him to share his Father with us. Friendship with him entails absolute loyalty on both sides. He, most readily, most devotedly, lays down his life for his friends. On the other hand, his friends never let him down. They are at his side in all his trials, never desert him whatever happens. They stand up before 'men' and acknowledge him, never allowing the opinions, fashions, ridicule or persecutions of 'men' to lead them to betray or deny their friend. And when we are his friends, how confidingly we can approach the Father.

Jesus teaches his friends a prayer that enshrines all he wants to teach them, all he asks of them. It is addressed to Abba. We are to say 'Our Father'. We know he is Father, not because we have proof, because, in the course of our lives we detect a fatherly care or because we often feel a warm loving presence; not because we see him granting our little wishes. No, we acknowledge him as Father for none of these reasons but simply because Jesus guarantees him. As with Jesus himself, everything can seem contrary to what we normally mean by father-love and care. By staking everything on Jesus' guarantee, and trying to live always in the faith that God is Father, we come to know that he is; that he is our ground, air, our encompassing, the source

17

of what we are and do. If we reflect carefully we shall find that we catch ourselves out in attitudes, words, actions, doubts, fears, scruples, that belie our notional belief. In actual fact, if not in 'belief', we are assuming that he is difficult to approach, that he is not concerned with us and has to be won over on to our side.

A friend told me of a little girl who was afraid when she woke up alone at night and frequently disturbed her parents by going along to them. 'But you are not alone', the mother reassured her, 'Jesus is with you'. 'I know,' her daughter replied, 'but I want someone with skin on.' This heartfelt vivid declaration echoes our own yearning. We find it so hard to 'live by faith alone', as we say. We too want someone 'with skin on'. The danger is that we try to put skin on. Misleading things are often said and written about the development of prayer and probably the outpourings of the mystics have been misinterpreted. Certainly we pick up the idea that sooner or later we shall realise the presence and love of God almost as though it were on the same level and mode of perception as human love. This is to overlook that our Abba is 'in heaven'. These are Jesus' words. Abba though he is, he is completely other, transcendent mystery. Between him and us there lies an unbridgeable gulf which we could never cross. He himself has thrown the bridge, his Jesus. Only because he has done this can we know him and the breathtaking truth that he calls us to intimacy. Our approach to him must always be with awe. 'O come, let us worship and bow down, let us kneel before the Lord, our maker!' Our whole being must be bowed in worship all day long. And we must renounce the desire to have a God we can handle. We can be like people at a seaside resort who prefer the man-made swimming pool with its easy temperature, safety and amenities. After all, it is sea-water! And a little beyond is the open sea, untrammelled, untameable, over which we have no control whatever. But it is to this sea that we must commit ourselves and let ourselves be carried away. It is terrifying, this immense sea that is God. What will he do with us? Where will he carry us? He is Abba, says Jesus. Fear not, trust him.

Faith is not a thing of the mind, it is not an intellectual certainty or a felt conviction of the heart, it is a sustained decision to take God with utter seriousness as the God of our life; it is to live out the hours in a practical, concrete affirmation that he is Father and he is 'in heaven'. It is a decision to shift the centre of our life from ourselves to him, to forgo self-interest and make his interests, his will our whole concern. This is what it means to hallow his name as Father in heaven. Often it may seem that we only act 'as if', so unaffected are our hearts, perhaps even mocking us: 'where is your God?' It is this acting 'as if' which is true faith. All that matters to faith is that God should have what he wants and we know that what he wants is always our own blessedness. His purposes are worked out, his will is mediated to us in the humblest form, as humble as our daily bread.

It is perhaps not too difficult to see God's providence in certain areas of our lives but it is likely that hour follows hour, full of little events, decisions and choices that are, in fact, divorced from him. If so we are denying him as Abba. We do not allow him to reign over us totally and we can excuse ourselves with the illusion that in our case the requisite conditions for total loving are not present. It would be different if such and such were different. Our situation is far too distracting and worrying. The truth is devastatingly simple and we are tempted to shirk the stark, overwhelming reality that God is giving himself to us in the stream of ordinary, mundane events in our ordinary, mundane life. This is where he is for us, here and not elsewhere. Here, precisely here, must we hallow his name. Nothing is wanting to us. 'Fresh and green are the pastures where he gives me repose.' It is not for us to judge whether they are fresh and green and sustaining. If he puts us there, even though they seem to us barren and hard, a place of struggle rather than repose, they are the pastures we need and in which we shall grow. We pray 'give us this day our daily bread'. When you pray, Jesus tells us, you have to believe your prayer is already heard. We cannot judge results. We are certain that everything that comes to us is our daily nourishing bread. This is what it means to believe: to take that daily bread and eat it with love and gratitude no matter how bitter the taste. By nature we, as it were, stand on the viewpoint of self and judge other people, things, what is happening, from that stand. Faith demands that we deliberately get off that stand and move to another, the viewpoint of Jesus, and then, how different everything looks! This needs constant effort, constant readjustment. Unless we undertake this battle against our subjectivity, how we feel, how things look to us and so forth, and choose to stand on Jesus and live our lives in his vision, we shall never get anywhere. And yet, how few do this day in day out until it is second nature, their own nature. These indeed have put on the mind of Christ.

Jesus bids us say 'Our Father' and to hallow his name must mean taking very seriously that everyone is a child of this Father and our brother or sister. As God's chosen ones, holy and beloved, we must put on compassion, kindness, lowliness, meekness and patience, forgiving one another . . . we must show constant, unconditional love and goodness to all no matter how they treat us because this is what God is like and does. He is forgiveness – a love always on tiptoe to give. As soon as we are there to receive he gives himself. We must be like this, we must respond to others like this. Unless we do so we cannot receive God's love. We have turned away from him. Nowhere, except when he is quoting the *Shema*, does Jesus speak of our loving the Father. He tells us we must believe in the Father, trust him, obey him, and love our neighbour. It can seem presumptuous to speak of loving God – as though we can! We love Jesus and he has spelt out for us what loving him means – keeping his commandments. This surrender to Jesus in keeping his words, immediately puts us in the Father's waiting embrace. 'If anyone loves me, he will keep my word, and my Father will love him'.[1] A loving fellowship is established. Jesus loves the Father. The Father loves Jesus. Only in Jesus can we love the Father and receive his love. We love the brother we see and his brothers living with us in our mortal life, and in doing so, we are loving the unspeakable mystery, the Father.

> O righteous Father, the world has not known thee, but I have known thee; and these have known that thou has sent me. I have made known thy name to them and will make it known, that the love with which thou hast loved me may be in them, and I in them.[2]

Sometimes we can feel as if life is just too hard, or just too uninteresting and drab. It can seem that the obstacles within ourselves are mountainous and insuperable. Jesus' own unwavering faith must be ours. Everything is possible to him who believes, was his humble boast. When everything seemed to be going wrong for him, when the 'no' of human hearts had congealed into hard rock which threatened to grind him down, he was certain that his Father could and would move that hard mass and drown it for ever. He died in hope, not in hopes realised. The picture of him asleep in the violent storm when others were frantic and angered by his seeming indifference reveals his inmost heart in its perfect trust. If we would be his friends we must live like that. A friend of Jesus dares all and never

[1] John 14:23.   [2] John 17:25–6 RSV.

says such and such is too hard. If God asks something then it is possible of accomplishment. His friends evade nothing, be it trying situations, uncongenial people, difficult duties. They take each day as it comes with its pleasures and joys, its disagreeable things and pains, shoulder their cross and go with Jesus. The significance of the cross is not suffering but obedience – doing the Father's will regardless of whether it is easy or hard.

For the true friends of Jesus evil does not exist. Everything is turned to good. Death itself, the epitome of all that is evil and destructive of man, is transformed. In his wonderful riposte to the Sadducees who denied the resurrection, Jesus, himself still in faith and not in sight, gloriously affirms our everlasting future, simply because he knows his Father and he knows this Father could never abandon his friends. The idea is unthinkable. 'You are quite, quite wrong,' he emphatically declares, and closes the issue.

Friends of God? Can it be? Yes, but there is only one way: to become 'son'; to accept the friendship and companionship of Jesus so as to learn sonship from him, share in his sonship. In practice this means being utterly unimportant to ourselves, becoming selfless, empty, nothing but an echo – like Enoch disappearing. This is the paradox: the one who has consented to be nothing but an emptiness for the Father's love, becomes – and only now, in this context of nothingness, dare we breathe the word – somehow 'equal' to God, raised up to be his friend, his beloved. 'The Father and I are one', says Jesus. Lost in his *kenosis* it can perhaps be said of us.

Our Father

Prologue

One of the profoundest ways of expressing our human vocation, and one that is truly biblical, is to say that we are called, each one of us, to be a son of God. (The word in our sense transcends gender.)

This expression carries within it almost all there is to say about what it means to be human. Man is truly man only when he is a son of God. And we know that this vocation of ours exists only in the perfect Son, Jesus Christ our Lord.

We do not become sons alongside him. No, it is into his sonship that we enter; the grace of his sonship is given to us. The Father sends the spirit of this one Son into our hearts, whereby we too cry 'Abba, Father'.[1]

My hope is that these reflections will sharpen our desire to receive this marvellous vocation and also point the way in. As our whole human vocation is enshrined for us in the Lord's Prayer we shall use it as both guide and inspiration.

[1] Rom. 8:15–16.

Our Father

'Go and find the brothers, and tell them: I am ascending to my Father and your Father, to my God and your God.'[1] This is the triumphant proclamation of the vindicated Jesus who lived and died in an ecstasy of love for his Father, Abba.

That God is Father is the heart of the gospel, it *is* the good news. Everything else derives from this, and not until Jesus came could we know it. True, other men had spoken of God as Father, but theirs was an uncertain knowledge, inevitably circumscribed by a purely human appreciation of the word.

Jesus' revelation of the Father is unique, and its implications not merely world-shaking but world-remaking. For Jesus, God's name, his true being, is precisely Father and nothing else. He alone is Father, and human fatherhood is but a shadowy reflection of his. 'Call no one on earth your father . . . you have only one Father and he is in heaven;'[2] if only we could thrust our brand into the fire of this truth and receive its power!

Paul burst out in a paeon of worshipful love: 'I fall on my knees to the Father of our lord Jesus Christ from whom all fatherhood (and motherhood) in heaven and on earth is named.'[3] We readily assume that this is merely a matter of attributing to God what we associate with *any* parenthood worthy of the name. Paul understands rightly that it is the other way round. God alone

[1] John 20:17. [2] Matt. 23:9. [3] Eph. 3:14 (freely translated).

is Father and thus it is he who is the norm for all human parenthood.

Jesus speaks to us of the Father's way, how the Father sees and estimates. He speaks of him as being absorbed in us, knowing all our needs, accounting for every hair of our heads. He is to be relied on absolutely, always there to receive us, enfolding us in tenderest, unconditional love.[1]

But the deepest revelation of the Father is Jesus himself, behind and beyond his words. It is not uncommon today to hear the objection that God as Father means nothing to many people, or is positively revolting because they have never known a father's love. If they have never experienced fatherly love how can they respond to the good news that God is Abba? Human love and its wondrous power of transformation should not be belittled; but never to have experienced parental affection, while it may leave a lifelong emotional void, need be no barrier to surrendering confidently to our Father in heaven. We do not have to seek an answer in human testimony; we look to Jesus, who in his own person shows us the Father. 'Call no one on earth your father . . . you have only one Father and he is in heaven'.[2]

We have, then, no excuse. True, our emotions may remain blocked and frozen, but nothing can stop us from growing in the knowledge of God our Father and living out that knowledge (which is all that matters). There must have been many times in Jesus' own life when what was happening to him seemed clean contrary to what, in our limited experience, we think of as fatherly love and care.

[1] Luke 12:1–32.   [2] Matt. 23:9.

It was by being Son that Jesus revealed Abba as he really is. Jesus understood that he could only be a perfect Son, allow the Father to beget him into all fullness, if he opened himself to receive, and receive at every moment of his life. It meant being totally dependent on the Father, accepting to have no life of his own, no rights, no initiatives. He existed by the Father, to receive the Father. And thus the Father was able to give everything to Jesus – 'all I have is yours'. In his turn Jesus could affirm, 'all I have is yours and all you have is mine'.[1] 'Everything has been entrusted to me by my Father.'[2]

So complete is the transaction, the self-bestowal of the Father, that only he can truly know Jesus; for who can know what God is save God himself?[3] And in consequence only Jesus knows the Father truly, the Father whose perfect reflection he is.[4]

Jesus' thoughts, words, actions, are those of the Father, and all can be summed up ultimately in saying that the Father communicates to him his own passion for us. This was the burden Jesus had to bear. His human finite heart had to receive this love and express it. At times the burden seemed insupportable: 'Oh faithless and perverse generation, how long am I to be with you. How long am I to bear with you?'[5] And yet he immediately summons the suffering boy after these words and cures him.

'Come to me all you who labour and are overburdened, and I will give you rest. Shoulder my yoke and learn from me, for I am gentle and humble in heart, and you will find rest for your souls. Yes, my yoke is easy and

---

[1] John 17:10.   [2] Luke 10:22.   [3] 1 Cor. 2:11.   [4] Heb. 1:3.
[5] Luke 9:41 (freely translated).

my burden light.[1] Jesus' own indestructible, unweary-
ing tender love and compassion are the Father's. What
Jesus does the Father is doing.

Jesus, instinct with the Father's will, shares his Father
with us. Solidly based on the rock of Abba-love, as
maternal as it is paternal, Jesus summons us to an obedience like his own. We must allow the Father to be truly
Father, to beget us, to communicate himself to us,
and this means the most profound self-abdication. Jesus
never said no, it was always yes, and amen. At each
successive moment of his humble suffering life he
surrendered to his Father, and thus the more his Father
could give. The climax was reached in the self-expenditure of the cross when his heart was broken open. This
was the fullest expression, such as we understand it
now, of total love.

Jesus trusted blindly; trusted when everything fell to
pieces around him. The Father would vindicate the Son
of his love. Faced with death he voiced his certitude
that the kingdom was at hand and, the ordeal over, he
would be drinking new wine with his disciples.[2] The
seed must die but the harvest would come[3] – how could
the Father not act, not vindicate his Son? But it must
be on the Father's terms, in the Father's own way.

The resurrection was the Father's divine answer. What
this means now to Jesus we cannot fathom; but this we
do know, that all Jesus stood for is true, that God is
Abba, and the only meaning of human life is to learn
what that means – to know with Jesus' own knowledge
and allow God to be Abba to us.

When you pray you must say 'Our Father. . .'[4]

[1] Matt. 11:28–30.   [2] Luke 22:18.
[3] John 12:24.   [4] Matt 6:9 (freely translated).

29

Who art in heaven

Father in heaven. We cannot separate these two concepts. The Father Jesus gives us is a 'holy Father', whom the world *cannot* know because it *will* not. Only Jesus can know him and those who humbly accept to share in his knowledge.[1]

If we are to know God it can only be because he chooses to reveal himself. Between him and us there is an unbridgeable gulf that we ourselves, of ourselves cannot cross. He is completely 'other', transcendent mystery, yet a mystery that draws near to us and lovingly beckons. It is he who has made the bridge across the abyss; he has opened a door into his own eternal being, and that door is Jesus.[2]

The 'world', that does not and cannot know God is human pride and self-sufficiency, the enemy of the God that really is. This world chooses to stand on itself, in a way of existence within its own bounds and control, and refuses the invitation to be drawn beyond itself into God's holy being. It resists with murderous panic the mystery that is Love. This world wants power over its god, wants to grasp him in the tentacles of knowledge, wants a puppet controlled by its own dictates – and this world is in us all.

For us to say in truth, 'Father in heaven', means we humbly receive our being from him, affirming that it is for *him* to design our destiny and for *him* to enable

[1] John 17.25.   [2] John 10.9.

us to achieve it. We deliberately surrender all attempts to control our own lives, to be our own captain. We must not dictate to God, demanding that he be the sort of God *we* want, nor must we prescribe a way for ourselves; rather we must allow ourselves to be led.

'In heaven' means God is hidden from our natural perception. This is an inescapable truth which our intellect is bound to acknowledge; but how hard it is to live by this truth consistently! We expend energy in an anxious search for tangible tokens, trying to catch glimpses of him, feel touches of his hand . . . our poor misguided hearts contrive little fantasies to reassure us in the silence and darkness. Even though our intellect would deny it, our hearts conclude when such tokens are lacking that God is difficult to approach, fearsome, or simply 'not there' for us.

Our perplexities, our anxieties and fretting, speak louder then words, that we think he is a fickle God, one who plays games with us, something of a sadist, who dumps us in a maze and from his vantage point above finds perverse satisfaction in our hopeless attempts to find our way. He does not help us, no matter how hard we pray.

The answer to this pathetic self-torture is simply Jesus. Jesus shows us a Father of tenderest caring who would gather us under his wings as a mother hen gathers her chicks.[1] A Father who in his holy love makes great demands but who has given us his Jesus, in whom and by whom we can fulfil those demands to our everlasting blessedness. All we need to know is Jesus, and base our lives on his dark knowledge of Abba. If only we could resolve once for all to do this and refuse all desire to

[1] Luke 13:34.

drag him into the light of day, to set ourselves up as the judges of his providence.

It is not for us to interpret the events of life in that we would presume to assert that *this* rather than *that* was God's intervention. It is true that most of us feel we can recognise his special providence in certain momentous happenings; but this should simply convince us of his continual providence always, all the time, and especially in those events and at those times when to our way of thinking we feel he has left us alone.

Likewise we cannot presume to know when he is closest to us at prayer: that *this* was a deep experience of him whereas *that* was his absence. Hidden God that he is he is infinitely near, *always* present in his loving self-bestowal, the ultimate controller and source of every-thing. All is worthy of him as Abba.

We are to be with him 'in heaven' and this means, among other things, that we too must be hidden. Our true self, our life in Jesus, is concealed even from ourselves. Can we accept this out of love for him?

Hallowed be thy name

We hallow God's name when we make our lives a continual acknowledgement that we have a Father in heaven. The full implications of this holy fatherhood must unfold as we grow in practical faith. Practical faith – in reality there is no other sort of faith. Faith is not faith unless it is on the move, so to speak. Faith is not something lodged in the head or even in the heart; it is an activity, something that is always in operation and grows stronger by exercise.

We belong to our holy Father, a hidden God, but in that hiddenness totally present. How then can we fritter away our lives as though they were unimportant? To be Father means to be life-giver, and God's deepest desire for us is fullness of life. We must want this too. We must want to live each moment of our lives, *really* live, not just undergo. This means hoarding jealously the opportunities for growth – they come, are offered, they pass and never come again. They can be exploited or lost for ever . . . unique opportunities of expressing our love and gratitude to him who so loves us . . . of blind trust in him whom at present we cannot see or enjoy. Alas, that we value our lives so little and waste numerous occasions!

God summons us to deepest intimacy with himself even in this life. We are bidden to whisper the filial intimate name 'Abba', that was Jesus' own name for him.[1] But this intimacy must be permeated with awe. That does

[1] Rom. 8:15–17.

not mean we have to work up a sensation of awe before the holiness and majesty of God. It does mean that we must never trifle with this God, never allow a substitute; rather we must dethrone, or allow him to dethrone, every idol we have set up, and the primal idol is our own self.

Jesus was smitten to the heart at the lack of gravity and seriousness he witnessed all around him, and that from people who professed belief in his Father. In practice the Father mattered little to them: their immediate satisfaction, their security, their comfortable complacency that they were on good terms with God, or conversely, their atheistic cynicism, mattered far more.

Jesus shows us what it is to hallow God's name. Not a moment of his precious life was frittered away, no occasion was lost, be it one of joy or sorrow. It was in the same situation as we are, a situation of inherited weakness, trouble and temptation, that Jesus hallowed the name of his Father, flashing back to him, as in an untarnished mirror, his own self-giving. In his deepest anguish he still murmured the tender name of 'Abba'.[1] His lips uttered it but his *whole* being was ratifying: 'You are my Abba, my holy Abba.'

It is within our own sinful context, not away from it, that we hallow God's name; when in temptation and conflict, in the misery of our bad moods, 'under' not 'on top', it is then that we must struggle to love if only by a feeble smile, refusing a criticism, even an interior one, struggling to be sensitive to another's feelings, to bite back a haughty rejoinder, allowing ourselves to be imposed upon. What priceless opportunities!

Holy Father, make me know you in a living way so

[1] Luke 23:46.

that I never pass you by, never slight you, but use every
moment to hallow your name.

Thy kingdom come

When we pray 'Thy kingdom come' we are inviting God to come and do in us all that he wants to do. We are affirming that we want him to be our God and Father, to love us into the fullness of life. We are praying that his great plan of love for his creation be accomplished. Nothing else can satisfy the human hearts he has made for himself. 'If you knew the gift of God',[1] Jesus cries; he who did know it and esteemed it truly.

If God is to be really our God and Father he must be allowed a free hand. He must reign. Ah, but *we* want to reign in the little world of our own life. We want to own ourselves and run our kingdom. We will fly God's flag, we will keep his laws as best we can, but hand over control? No, that we cannot do! It would mean losing everything, ceasing to be human, for after all, autonomy is our inalienable right. It is the way we are, the way we live and function.

Pray 'Thy kingdom come', says Jesus, 'surrender to that kingdom, it is your blessedness. You think you will lose your life? Believe me, you will gain it, your only true life, eternal life.'[2] The kingdom is fully present in Jesus for he has allowed God to be his God, his Abba.

The kingdom is pure gift, the pure, gracious self-giving of the God of love. We can never take hold of it, never

[1] John 4:10 RSV.   [2] Matt. 10:39.

36

bring it in, cannot even know of its existence. To see it, to enter in, we must be born again of water and spirit.[1]

The water of our natural being, no matter how fertile it seems, is mere chaos until it is touched by the Spirit. God alone can bring to realisation its rich potential. We must yield to him, recognise our chaos, and long to become the garden, the domain of God.

From a careful reading of the gospel of John comes an almost devastating impression of Jesus as emptied out; an impression of what it means for a man to let God rule him absolutely, to let God be God – and Father. Over and over he insists that nothing comes from himself, it is all received. Too easily we interpret the sayings of Jesus in a diametrically opposite way. We conclude he had a sense of his own grandeur and 'Godness', a luminous, cloudless knowledge, a sense of walking in a higher, unearthly dimension, aware of power within him, rich in inner resources. His hearers accused him of boasting and blasphemy because they too misunderstood.

From the depths of his self-emptied being Jesus could make unrivalled affirmations: 'I am the light of the world';[2] 'I am resurrection and life';[3] 'the Father and I are one'.[4] He has let God give, has let God hand over everything to him as a true father does.[5]

In reality Jesus was crying out: 'You don't understand. I am claiming nothing for myself. I am absolutely nothing, I have no resources. I am the poorest of the poor, I am no-self, but the Father is all to me and in

[1] John 3:5.   [2] John 8:12.   [3] John 11:25.
[4] John 10:30.   [5] John 13:3.

me, and that is why I am his living presence among you.'

'Come, learn of *me*', he says, 'and you will find rest.'[1] First of all we must admit that only God can purify and transform us. This is said easily enough but in practice we do not think so. We insist on running our own spiritual life, we get worked up when things go wrong (according to our ideas), we are pleased with ourselves when we feel good and successful.

We are inflexible with our own concept of God, how he is and how he should act. We initiate and decide, and then think it is up to him to comply and applaud. Or we make a mess of things and see him as displeased, threatening (albeit mildly).

'Thy kingdom come'! Let us pray it blindly, not knowing really what we are asking, and over and over again, several times a day, explicitly tell him we intend that he shall have everything, he shall be allowed to do all he wants to do. This basic intention we must keep before us and be always looking at him, seeing what he wants here and now and giving it. If we keep our inner eyes on him – and maintaining a sincere intention is precisely that – we shall not miss him. We shall be so busy with him that we shall forget our own ideas and plans. We cannot be taking our own initiatives at the same time as we are bent on waiting for his.

We are utterly confident that the Father wants to give us his kingdom[2] and that he will leave no stone unturned to do so. There is no need for strain or anxiety. There is no mysterious art to be mastered, it is all there before us at each moment. What God asks of us we can always

[1] Matt. 11:28 (freely translated).   [2] Luke 12:32.

accomplish. There is nothing to be afraid of. It is not a chancy thing that might not come off.

Be happy to feel that you cannot control your life, that there is so much in you that you seem unable to cope with. Trust yourself to him, take each moment as it comes, for each moment holds him. Let him have the say, let him take charge, even though you are left feeling that no one is in charge.

Dispossession of self is the reverse side of God-possession.

Thy will be done

Jesus the perfect Son was a completely obedient man who always did his Father's will right to the end.[1]

He surrendered to every manifestation of God's will no matter how concealed its origin – in darkness, in pain. Now he tastes, experiences through and through what it means to be Son; what it means to have a God who is Father. He has been perfected, he has reached fulfilment.

The Father asks for perfect obedience only because openness to him, surrender to his essentially mysterious working, is the only way the human creature can be brought to perfect fulfilment – which is perfect happiness.

What we have seen Jesus doing in relation to his Father we must do in our turn. When we look at the Jesus of the gospels we see a man devoured by love and devotion towards God, his Father. It is a devotion expressed in act by absolute submission and obedience. It is a practical love of complete self-expenditure.

The Father alone mattered to Jesus. He did not matter to himself at all. He left it to his Father to care for him; his whole substance was expended for him. Jesus was so given, so surrendered, so emptied out, that he was like a hollow shell in which the roar of the ocean could

[1] John 8:29.

40

be heard. He was an emptiness in which the Father could fully express his own self-giving being.

We have to be living embodiments of Jesus, as he is of the Father. And this, says Jesus, is joy: 'My joy which you must share.'[1]

It is Jesus who reveals what it means to be human. He is the light on the otherwise incomprehensible mystery of man. Now that he is the risen Lord he knows whence he comes. He knows with the fullness of knowledge, in the full light of day and face to face, the Father from whom he draws his being, his meaning, his completion. He has reached his term, the goal of his developing, striving being – the Father.

Jesus has become his completed self, perfect Son, by living entirely in, on, from, for the Father. He is therefore Man, for the only meaning of man is to be a total 'for-Godness', son of God in the fullest meaning of the term son.

And each of us has to become Jesus. This is the Christian's sole aim which is nothing other than the destiny of all people; it is what human beings are for, what the world is for. This is the essence of all effective apostolate – to live the depth and breadth of the human vocation.

When we say 'Jesus' we are holding together two profound realities. We mean the living Lord in the glory of his victory, the surrendered One who is all God's. Our roots are in this victorious One. He is the ground on which we stand, the unshakeable rock, our perfect security.

But the risen Jesus is lost to our human gaze. He too

[1] John 15:11 (freely translated).

is in light inaccessible which our poor earthly sight cannot cope with. And we are not meant to try. Standing on his victory, drawing our life from his inexhaustible well-spring, we are gently turned away from him in splendour to contemplate him in his mortal existence. This is what we are doing when we meditate on the gospels. This is how we meet him, learn from him. We learn from him in the days of his flesh, when he too must contemplate the mystery of the Father, not face to face but in a mirror darkly as we do.[1]

He stood in tears, bruised by harsh reality as we are, searching for his Father's hand in the darkness, trusting to the Father's love when everything seemed contrary to it.

Jesus knew what was in man. His parables show that: human craftiness and meanness, hypocrisy, complacency, worldly-mindedness, unforgivingness, apathy! When we read how he was surrounded by the crowd – the palsied, the lame, the blind, the deaf, those controlled by demons – then we see what his living knowledge of human beings, his fellow men, was like.

But it is in the midst of this terrible awareness that he points us to the Father: 'Believe in God, believe also in me.'[2] Believe in me even though all I am affirming contradicts your sense of life.

From this Jesus we learn to live day by day our human vocation to be 'for-God'. All our judgements not ours but his; knowing only with his knowledge; no desire or will of our own but his, no power, no achievements. What Jesus was to his Father, we are to Jesus. 'As I live by the Father so you must live by me.'[3]

[1] 1 Cor. 13:12. [2] John 14:1 RSV. [3] John 6:57.

42

Thy will be done.

From the moment we get up each morning we must set our compass steadily in one direction. Moment by moment we must re-set it when it has veered away. Thoughts, words, deeds, must have one sole direction and must be corrected and brought to heel when they follow an alien track.

Only this constant hourly effort to live wholly in Jesus for God the Father is worthy of a Christian. And as we labour God is doing his part and transforming us at a depth we can never comprehend or even know is there.

On earth as in heaven

God wills our perfect fulfilment in him. He wills this absolutely and unchangingly. Everything is ordained to this. So to do his will means co-operating with him to bring this about.

This earth, all that goes to make up human history, is where the self-bestowal of God takes place. To attempt to escape from the earth and create a sort of spiritual 'heaven' where we can live a life more worthy of the spiritual beings we fancy we are, is to cut ourselves off from constant exposure to God and his transforming action.

We can hardly overstress the gravity of time and the realism with which we must take this world as the place where God reveals and gives himself to us. He is nowhere else. He is not away in heaven. He is with us; and therefore we are in heaven in the measure in which we allow him to give himself.

In the story of the transfiguration we see how the three disciples were given a glimpse, expressed in symbolic imagery, of the inner reality of Jesus, the Jesus they experienced in everyday clothes and with his Galilean accent. The Jesus who knew temptation, weariness, frustration. The Jesus who did ordinary things, who had worked as a carpenter and had an inside knowledge of village life. Now they saw this humble being radiant with God's own light, 'in heaven'.[1]

[1] Matt. 7:1–8; Mark 9:2–8; Luke 9:28–36.

God wills that heaven should invade earth, that earth should be transformed into heaven. This happens only when individual hearts allow him to triumph in them. Where he fully indwells there is heaven. This is what we are praying for when we ask that his will be done on earth as in heaven. It would be God's dear wish that there were no bit of earth that was just pure earth with no intermingling heaven. He would want each human earth to be heaven, his own dwelling place.

I saw
    the mist was deep and everywhere
    delicate though
    all one with the gossamer lace
        on the phantom bush
    pricked out with white-fired dew –

that all must be as it is

    So, kiss the soaked earth,
    lift your face to the luminous shroud.
    Walk in the Mist unshod.

Give us this day our daily bread

The great and holy will of God to give himself to you and me is mediated like the sun's rays. The pure white light is broken up into multiple particles. It reaches me in the here and now of all that happens in my daily life.

Give us this day our daily bread – give us the kingdom. What else can this mean but the kingdom perfect and whole? And God hears the prayer which he himself inspires.

Do I believe this? Do I see in what he gives me true bread? Do I take it humbly and gratefully and nourish myself on it? Or do I ignore it because it does not look like bread, does not taste like bread? 'What father among you would hand his son a stone when he asked for bread? Or hand him a snake instead of a fish? Or hand him a scorpion if he asked for an egg?'[1]

But we are quite capable of thinking our heavenly Father does this sort of thing which the most ordinary of fathers would never do. Can we not in obscurity, in faith, believe? Must everything satisfy sense and intellect before we bow our heads in submission?

To act like this is not faith. It is the way of the flesh, that flesh which is like the flower of the field, lacking all substance.[2]

When it comes down to it the proof of faith lies in how

[1] Luke 11:12.   [2] Isa. 40:6–8.

we view our daily lives. Do we see all as the holy bread our Father gives us? His pure will coming to us in this unexpected event; this lowly service?

We have to accept him in the life and circumstances he has given us, and this we find so appallingly hard. We want another sort of life that is more interesting, circumstances that tune in more with what we think God's coming should be like.

I came across the statement that Mark's gospel is wholly concerned with the secret epiphanies of God, and this struck me, for I see it reflects perfectly our own situation. Mark shows us Jesus as naked man: he is moved to anger, grief, horror, fear, he manifests ignorance, he dies helplessly calling out in dereliction. At the same time Mark succeeds in showing him as divine: the Father acknowledges him, others become fleetingly aware of the presence of the numinous in him, he works miracles.

But if we look at these miracles we find that people as a whole were not convinced by them. It was only the perceptive heart – and that of unlikely people – not his own relatives, not his own race, not even his disciples, who saw something of the truth. The epiphany was hidden and yet it *was* an epiphany. Here, it seems to me we have the kernel of it.

Every minute of life contains these secret epiphanies. If we live continually in their ambience then indeed we live by faith. If everything is such an epiphany for us then our faith is perfect.

God is coming to us all the time but we do not hold ourselves attentive to meet him, to receive him and to give him what he wants. His coming is as lowly, as commonplace, as without thrills as our daily bread.

47

When Jesus was a grown man, when he stood on the brink of his passion at the end of his short life spent in utter self-giving, he did a simple human thing. He took material elements, food and drink which in themselves symbolise human life; he prayed to his Father to ratify what he was doing, and he gave this food and drink to his disciples with the words: 'My body for you. . . The new covenant in my blood for you. . . Do this in memory of me.'[1]

The bread and wine signified his own perfect offering, lifelong, from the cradle onwards, and soon to be summed up finally in his surrender to death. Rightly has the Church seen that in fulfilling his will – 'Do this in memory of me' – she is precisely re-enacting the mystery of his total self-oblation. Through this sacrament the Church puts herself in the presence of this mystery, makes it hers: it becomes *for us* our daily bread.

So her children bring the bread and wine, fruit of the earth, work of their hands, symbols of the offering of ourselves. These are laid upon the altar with our poor lives, each day, each hour . . . filled with little actions, aspirations, fears, longings, sufferings – all that goes to make up a human span – but in sacrifice. We want these poor earthly things to be an expression of perfect love for the Father.

We give you, dear Lord, all we have and are under the veil of bread and wine. In themselves, as of themselves, they are ineffective, they can never carry us to the Father. Make them into your own offering, your own flight of love which does get there. Transform us into your immolated self.

[1] Matt. 26:26–9; Mark 14:22–5; Luke 22:17–19.

In Holy Communion we receive back the humble offerings we first presented, not as themselves, but as sacrament of union, of transformation. We eat God and are transformed thereby. Not so that we become something marvellous but so that we become nothing but a living response, an act of obedience, a pure burnt offering. Thus we too will shine with the light of Godhead – but he alone will see it.

Give us this day our daily bread – the bread of your will, the bread of your body.

Forgive us our trespasses

'Forgive us our wrong doing.' Our Lord, who puts these words on our lips, is the atonement for them. We do not have to *earn* forgiveness or *make* it: we have only to take advantage of what is already there, what has been done for us.

Sin is not a thing; it is not a moral stain or blemish, it is a damage to a relationship, a rejection of love. It is a gap, a chasm, and those who have chosen to be far off must be brought close.

It is God himself who brings about this reconciliation, this reunion, this at-one-ment. Jesus' coming has simply everything to do with the forgiveness of sins. The good shepherd comes himself to search for the lost sheep and bring him home.[1]

'Jesus Christ came into the world to save sinners'[2] – this is an absolutely true saying, states the Epistle to Timothy. Thus we are certain of forgiveness, that God never holds our sins against us. 'It is a joy, a bliss, an endless satisfying to me, that ever I suffered passion for thee,'[3] wrote the medieval mystic Julian of Norwich in her penetrating way, placing these words on the lips of Jesus. Yes, but should *we* take this 'blissful passion' lightly?

Truly there is a terrible cost to be borne, but it is he,

[1] Luke 15:4–7.   [2] 1 Tim. 1:15.
[3] *Revelations of Divine Love*, ch. 22.

not us, who bears it. We need to ponder this cost lest we underestimate our infidelity, soothing ourselves with, 'he understands . . . others may condemn me, but he understands'; in the sense that he does not think much of my shabbiness and lack of generosity.

'He came to save sinners of whom I am the greatest.' Can we say that sincerely? Well, if we think of sin in terms of adultery, murder, extortion and the rest, of course we cannot say we are the greatest of sinners. But if we put sin in the right context, that is in the context of relationships, of surrender to the love of God, then I do not think we shall have any difficulty, provided we are close enough to him to realise just how mediocre, mean and shabby we are. We have been given 'much'.[1] and therefore our small 'noes' are infinitely more significant than the objectively 'big' sins of others. Yet we too are forgiven, everything can be put right, the relationship not only restored but enhanced.

An awareness of our sinfulness is part of holiness; you simply cannot have holiness without it for it is the inevitable effect of God's closeness. This is why true sorrow for sin is never morbid, depressed; for it carries with it the certainty of forgiveness.

The keenest sense of our guilt is thus bound up with the unfailing certainty of pardon; and the deepest contrition excludes all discouragement by renewing childlike trust. We should want compunction like this with all our hearts.

Scripture assures us that Jesus comes to heal our blindness, and blindness in regard to sin is our chief blindness. To a great extent, perhaps wholly, we choose

[1] Luke 12:48.

how much we see. We cannot have God unless we are prepared to see ourselves, our lives, our past and present as they are, and half-consciously we know this revelation would be terrible. Therefore we make a choice not to see, or not to see very much.

Come and enlighten us, Sun of holiness. Show us our sloth, our pride, our shirking of the demands of life, our evasions. Reveal to us our sinfulness in the light of your mercy, and then we shall be healed and know perfect joy.

Let us ask the Lord to break once for all the chain that keeps us captive in darkness – not total darkness, for after all we are children of the day[1] – but partial darkness, not the full radiance of his light.

This particular aspect of our Lord's coming to us as a healer of our sinfulness is 'held' for us in a sacrament, a special 'moment'. As always with a sacrament there is a wedding of the human and the divine. Our part is to take our act of sorrow, paltry and inadequate as it is, to that heart which alone has gauged sin, taken its full weight. Our poor sorrow is taken up into, transformed into, the perfect reparation of Jesus.

'People of Sion weep no more.'[2] Nothing is wanting to you. Every one of your needs is supplied. 'Comfort, comfort my people.'[3] Bring to me in this sacrament not a detailed list of your faults but the whole expanse of your sinfulness which I see but as yet you do not. Let me deal with it. Be prepared to be enlightened at whatever cost; be prepared to take practical steps when light dawns.

When we run to our Father's arms in this sacrament we

[1] 1 Thess. 5:5.   [2] Isa. 30:19.   [3] Isa. 40:1.

take the whole sinful but dearly-loved world with us. We hear the certain assurance: 'I forgive.' All our wrongs by him are righted. The Church is built up again, her broken walls restored in full.

Many of us, I think, were we to analyse our attitude to confession, would find our lack of zeal regarding it due to the sheer poverty of the rite. We are aware of the utter paltriness of our confession and sorrow. But this is just the point. The more paltry the better. It is Jesus' atoning love, his sorrow, that are going to matter.

And on the other side there is just a human voice speaking the words of absolution. Nothing to strike the senses, nothing whatever!

And how appropriate! When Jesus came to deal with sin what was there to see? 'And here is a sign for you: you will find a baby wrapped in swaddling clothes'.[1] No sign at all if you mean a striking verification: but a perfect sign if we mean a sacrament, a manifestation in the flesh, in human terms, of God's perfect self-giving coming to us where we are, as we are, born to all the burdens of a sinful world.

[1] Luke 2:12.

As we forgive others

Our Lord shows us that we simply cannot be in a position to receive forgiveness unless we recognise our need for it, unless we know we are sinners. And once we know we are sinners we simply cannot refuse to forgive our neighbour.

To be unforgiving to my neighbour means in fact that I have no idea of my sinfulness, or at least that I refuse to admit that I am a sinner. Unforgivingness springs from the desire to feel better than another, to have an ascendancy, to have rights.

An acceptance of ourselves as sinners in the light of knowing that Jesus is all for sinners, that he is reconciliation, is incompatible with insisting on our rights, wanting power and control over others, wanting to feel better than they are.

When we stop to think about it, which of us has ever been 'wronged' in an objective sense? What we usually mean when we say we feel wounded and hurt is that someone has not treated us with the thoughtfulness and consideration we think is our due. Someone has not acted as *we* think right and as *we* want.

In other words, in practice forgiving others usually means nothing more than allowing others to be different. It is the fact that others are different that jars and irritates us. We talk about them wronging us, being unfair to us, and all we mean is that they do not conform to our pattern.

You would think it would be easy for us to accept this, but it is not, as our Lord makes clear. It is one of the few specific commands he laid upon us – forgive absolutely, for only in this way are you in the disposition to receive your Father's forgiveness.[1] And to receive God's forgiveness is to receive God: it is union, the Father drawing us closer to himself, as in the parable of the prodigal son.[2]

Forgiveness, mercy, self-abasement, are divine concepts. We learn from Jesus that they are of the very essence of God, and when he tells us that we must be perfect as our heavenly Father is perfect it is in direct reference to these precise qualities of God. We must be totally, utterly good to others regardless of how they treat us.[3]

Jesus says that our Father will not forgive us unless we forgive each other from our hearts. It is not that he *will* not but that he *cannot*. An unforgiving heart is a heart closed to receiving the rivers of Christ's redemptive love.

We should see great significance in our Lord's constant references to the matter of forgiving others. Clearly he felt this was one of the basic obstacles to his Father's love. Looking back at our past perhaps we have to admit with shame that we sometimes retaliated and tried to hurt back, but with the passing of years and the mellowing of age we say we have forgiven and mean it. Yet so often, if we are honest, we surprise ourselves under pressure. We rake up from the past incidents we had long buried . . . buried, yes, but not really forgiven. Our Lord knows how hard it is for the self-protective human heart to forgive totally.

[1] Matt. 6:14–15.   [2] Luke 15:11–24.   [3] Matt. 5:43–8.

For me the most helpful reflection is one which has been borne out as truth over and over again by experience. We have touched on it once already. It is that what we are asked to forgive is nothing more or less than that other people are 'other' – not me, different from me, with a whole range of different patterns of thinking, reacting. I must offer other people unconditional forgiveness for their otherness, their 'you-ness' when their 'you-ness' bumps up against and bruises my 'me-ness'. Perfect 'me-ness' lies not in self-protection but in exposure – in loving, giving, mercy, self-abasement.

It seems to me that if we reflect long and hard on the matter in these terms and determine to act accordingly we have shut the door on the enemy for ever.

No one then will wrong us. We shall never have anything to brood over, get angry about, hurt about, and ache to revenge in some petty way. Revenge is a dreadful sin in a follower of Jesus, and yet its malice can be hidden by its pettiness.

If we peacefully allow others to be 'other' we shall be doing precisely what Jesus bade us: 'Do not judge.'[1]

'Do not judge' because you simply cannot know the truth about someone else's motives. Only God can know the mysterious depths of the human heart. When we judge, what we are actually saying is that if *I* did or said so and so it would be because I was angry, jealous etc. But we presume to add, they do this therefore *they* are angry, jealous etc. They mean to hurt me.

By making a habit based on Jesus' teaching (but also on common sense and experience), of reflecting that we

[1] Matt. 7:1.

56

simply cannot know another's motives, we are forced into making acts of blind trust in our neighbours, and that is wonderful.

I am convinced that this resolution, consistently practised, produces a pure, constant, tender love for all. What greater blessing could we wish for, and what better way to ensure our openness to Jesus so that he can use us as channels of his love.

Lead us not into temptation

In the stresses and strains of his mortal life, and in the uncontrolled pressures of brute forces, Jesus learned obedience. He learned, in other words, what it is to be Son and have a Father.[1]

No matter what the circumstances, no matter what the pressure or bitterness, Jesus loved. And in this he offered to his Father the sacrifice of perfect trust, devotion, obedience. He too must have been bewildered at what was happening, tempted to feel blind fate was governing his life and not the merciful, faithful Father he thought he knew.

'Tempted as we are'.[2] Does our Father lead us into temptation?

We know how the Old Testament overlooked all secondary causes and saw God as the direct agent of all that happened, good and bad. 'I am God unrivalled . . . the author of peace, the author of calamity'.[3] God hardened Pharoah's heart.[4] He shut the spiritual eyes and ears of people so that they could not see, could not hearken and so turn and be saved.[5]

These are strange words and we are loath to take them literally. We have reacted by giving due weight to secondary causes, thus preserving the freedom of man.

[1] Heb. 5:7–9.   [2] Heb. 2:18.
[3] Isa. 45:7 (freely translated).   [4] Exod. 7:3.
[5] Isa. 6:10.

We see that the evil in the world is largely due to man's wrong choices, to his blindness and mistakes. So conscious are we of natural causes that we are in danger of losing the vision of faith, obscured as events are by plausible explanations of causality.

Yet, with eyes wide open to every other consideration, we must still in faith say that God is in all, behind all, the ultimate cause. It is mystery, but a mystery we have to live with if we would stand in the truth.

If we dwell on this we are led to live our lives with the greatest attention. Wake up, says Scripture, be on the watch, loins girt, lamps burning, waiting for the Lord, ready to open to him when he knocks.[1]

This is the Christian attitude flowing from profound faith. God is always present, offering himself in one disguise or another. But we are not always on the watch and therefore we miss him, refuse to recognise him, and see only this inconvenience, that annoying person, and so forth.

Unless we have a faith that is continually watchful we do not advert to temptation. We are asleep. The temptation is precisely to sleep, not to recognise when we are being given a choice. The danger lies not so much in our saying a deliberate no to God asking something of us – if we are unfortunate enough to do this we know it and are sorry. The danger is that we are asleep and do not see what we are being offered so do not realise that we are saying no.

Lead us not into temptation. . . Keep us awake so that we always recognise you and say yes to you. Do not

1 Matt. 24:42; 25:1–13.

59

allow us to let the moments, hours, days, slip by with their countless encounters with you unheeded.

You will not fail us, help us not to fail you.

O God, my loving friend and my protector. What can I feel but confidence?

But deliver us from evil

Do not let evil overwhelm us. Do not let anything fall upon us that is too heavy for us to bear. Deliver us from evil.

There is only one evil – human selfishness. The basis of all sin is egocentricity. The whole movement of self-orientation has to be reversed.

God wills it to be reversed because only in this surrender of self-seeking and self-possession can he possess us, and thus become our fulfilment and happiness.

To combat evil in the world, to correct the balance in the world, the first thing anyone must do is to attack the evil in himself, to combat his own selfishness. In other words, each of us must learn to love. There is no other answer to the world's distress than this.

One of the principle truths of the mystery of our redemption is that the only real evil is sin: sin being understood as everything in us that is not transformed into God, everything whatsoever that opposes him – sin understood as a rejection of God.

All that we experience as evil – sickness, pain, death, calamity, war, violence and the cruel treatment of men, failure, brokenheartedness, mental illness – these we may not call evil in any ultimate sense.

Were it not for our redemption they would be evil indeed. For the natural man, for those who have no hope, they *are* evil. Likewise we too actually experience them as evil. The fact that our faith knows their inner meaning is transformed does not immunise us from their terrible effects on mind and body, but it does mean we are never crushed by them.

The evil effects of sin have become the path to glory. This is victory indeed!

Nothing, nothing whatsoever can separate us from the love of Christ: neither tribulation nor distress, persecution, famine, war, being without food, clothing or shelter . . . in all things we are more than conquerors through him who has granted us his love.[1]

O cross of Christ, your victory is ours. In your strength we lay hold of eternal life!

[1] Rom. 8:35–7 (freely translated).

Amen

Jesus is the great amen to all the promises of God,[1] to all that the Father has it in his heart to do, that Father who is the primal amen to creation begotten of his love, the God of amen.

·The Father is the absolute guarantor of our being. His loving designs towards us are unchanging, and, states the Epistle to the Hebrews, he longs to convince us, the heirs of the promise, of his unshakeable will to bring us to our perfect fulfilment in him.[2]

The Father entrusts amen to Jesus. Jesus takes this amen to himself, into his very being. He becomes amen: a total response and affirmation of all the Father wills.

Mysteriously significant is his unique habit of prefacing statements with amen. 'Amen, amen I say to you', stressing an authority which derives solely from the fact that he receives all from the Father, the supreme Amen. He does not initiate: he waits, listens, receives, obeys.

He had no blueprint of the Father's plans. His listening, his obedience, happened in the same human context as must ours. The present moment – what did it offer, what did it ask? As with us, it was like weaving a tapestry wrong side up with no seeming pattern. Jesus did not ask to see a pattern. He left that to his Father. His simple but all-demanding task was to be there,

[1] 2 Cor. 1:20.   [2] Heb. 5:9.

amen, the faithful and true witness, the beginning of God's creation.[1]

God willed to bring many sons to glory,[2] and to be son, to be human in the truest sense, is to be filled with the fullness of God.

Jesus was destined to be the Son, the Man, perfect reflection of the Father. He became the beginning, source of a new creation, through his labour of obedience.

And, says Paul, we utter our amen through him to the glory of God.[3] Because of him we too can become amen to all the promises of God, faithful and true witnesses to the everlasting, unshakable, invincible love of the Father.

[1] Rev. 3:14.   [2] Heb. 2:10.   [3] 2 Cor. 1:20.